EVERYDAY

Joy

Stop living for the weekend and start loving your everyday life

A 90-Day Journal

ALEXIS PIERCE

DEDICATION

To the woman I was in 2009 and to the woman
I didn't know I was becoming.

CONTENTS

ACKNOWLEDGMENTS

This journal was born of unlikely characters — desperation, anguish, hopelessness, powerlessness, and fear. Through these pages, a new cast was born — hope, love, faith, courage, passion, and above all, joy.

To those who stayed through all the acts, thank you.
Get ready for one heck of an after party.

DID I MENTION I WAS MISERABLE?

He left the bedroom in silence and returned with a condom. I laughed, *"You don't need that. I'm not having sex with you!"* After all we were just friends — co-workers, really. Ten minutes later, I fled to the bathroom, locked the door, and sat on the edge of the tub scared, dazed, and angry. That's how my breakdown began. It was May 2009.

Within months, I'd switched to a different job so I wouldn't have to see him again. The wheels were in motion for me to eventually leave my career as a high-level government strategist, but it would take another 17 months to play out. A year to the day of the incident, I sold my house and started house-sitting full time. By May 2011, I had left the government and was embarking on my new life alone on a mountain-top in northeastern New Zealand on 66 acres overlooking the ocean.

I never intended for my life to take such a fast and wild turn — or to leave my dream job so abruptly. I'd aspired to work in global peace since I was eleven years old puffy painting anti-war slogans on canvas bags. In the government, I'd worked my way up into an elite team of strategists who helped countries stabilize to prevent or recover from war. My passion for the work outweighed the doubts of my superiors, and soon enough I had been given the green light to create my own office and flag a team of experts ready to deploy within hours to advise flailing governments. It was everything I ever dreamed of. But even your greatest dreams can fall short of making you happy, and that's what happened with mine.

This journal was a tool I created during one of the hardest years of my life to help me find my way back to joy — back to myself.

I'd always known I would eventually leave the government. I had hopes of writing self-help books and empowering people to follow their passion. But change is hard, and I enjoyed being one of the top in my field and the recognition and awards that came with it. I felt important. My job title impressed my parents' friends back home. Sure, my heart wanted more, but I couldn't convince myself to make the leap.

So Life did what Life does; it nudged me along through pain to accentuate and accelerate my decision. Being assaulted by a colleague and friend woke me up, but I still had a long journey to find the clarity, strength, and confidence to leave my career and life in D.C..

During the year between leaving my dream job and leaving the government all together, I found myself counting the minutes until the end of each work day. When I was pasting on a fake smile until quitting time Friday, and then cursing Sunday for coming too soon, the questions in these pages helped me remember that every day in my life matters. They reminded me that Tuesday is just as important and special as Saturday, because both of those days are *my* life. In my eagerness for the "freedom" of the weekend, I was unknowingly wishing away the majority of my time. This journal brought me back to the magic and possibility — to the happiness — that is available now.

*

The first version of this journal was hand written in an 8 X 10" day planner I kept next to my bed. I also created one as a gift for a women in my trauma counseling group using colored pens with silver permanent marker on the cover. The journal had changed my life for the better, so I hoped it would help improve hers too.

Ten years later, I'm thrilled to finally be making this process available to more people. As a spiritual mentor and soul purpose guide, I've seen first-hand how much these questions have helped my clients and students reclaim a sense of self and step into greater confidence and daily happiness.

★

You don't have to feel like you're falling apart to benefit from this journal, though it's okay if you feel like you are. I've used this process to open my heart to more happiness, to feel more grateful and build my self-trust, and to rewire my brain to celebrate what I have, instead of focusing on what I don't have. That may sound like a tall order, but it works. Here's why:

Everyday Joy **retrains your brain to prioritize both yourself and your joy.**

That may not seem very revolutionary, but just think for a moment about your normal, everyday thoughts. Chances are your incredible brain power is caught up repeating the same few thoughts about the same daily annoyances and challenges Monday through Sunday. But your mind can do anything! It's like a super smart Labrador Retriever that can hunt down whatever you ask for at any moment. Which means, instead of focusing on how bad other drivers are or how much you wished your boss would see your value, you can unleash your mind on the scent of joy and lean back as it brings you the evidence of happiness in your life.

This is how you rewire your brain, and your whole life, for joy.

This journaling process does something else, too. Something I didn't anticipate when I first started using it in 2009. It builds your self-esteem.

By focusing every single day on YOU, you start to forge a better relationship with yourself. You start putting yourself and your happiness first. This simple shift creates ripples through your psyche and sends the message that you're paying attention, you care, and you're on Team YOU.

Even if right now you don't feel connected to yourself, confident in your choices, or able to trust your intuition, commit to using this daily journal. These questions will help you build a more loving and trusting relationship with yourself. These are your first steps to a whole new, happier way of being.

2

MAKING THE MOST OF YOUR
JOY JOURNAL

This journal is designed to be straight-forward and simple to use. You can get started right away and pick it up again at any time, even if you missed a few days. Over the next few pages, I share a few helpful hints and tips that will make the process even more effective for you.

Before you continue, take a moment right now to download the special meditations and bonus materials that accompany this journal. These will help you open to deeper levels of joy and appreciation for yourself and your life. You can access them at www.becomingyouniversity. com/everyday-joy-gifts.

Tip #1 - The daily celebration question is about choice.

The daily question asks you *how will you celebrate?* not how *could*, *should*, or *might* you celebrate. This is important and intentional. When you write your answer, say to yourself "*I will....*" This is powerful confirmation to your mind that you are actively choosing to celebrate and it is already happening.

Why it matters

Most of us go down a shame-and-blame spiral as soon as we start to do something good for ourselves. Ideally, you would actively choose a new habit because it feels good or you desire the outcome. Instead, you may pressure yourself to be better or different by telling yourself you really *should* be kinder or more patient or a better listener. The subtle implication is that you are not good enough, you are supposed to be better, and that any change you make is just closing the gap between who you are and who you already should be (if only you were better and perfect).

After years of personally trying that approach, I can confidently report that guilting, shaming, and pressuring yourself into being better doesn't work. It just leads to more guilt and shame. Instead, to create lasting change and shift into new, inspiring ways of being, I invite you to make a powerful choice in the present moment. *I will*....

Tip #2 - A celebration can be as big or as small as you'd like.

Whether you had a banana with lunch or spoke up for yourself in a tough situation, your celebration is a dedicated act of self-love - even if you weren't thinking about it in the moment (*more on that in Tips 3 & 4*). Your celebration can be anything, as long as it makes you feel good when you imagine it as an uplifting gift you're giving to yourself.

I can't say what a celebration might be for you because it's inherently personal; it's what feels nourishing and loving for you. For example, if you go to the gym but your sole focus is losing weight and saying that you worked out, then you may be acting from a feeling of pressure or guilt. But if you're at the gym to connect with your body, clear your mind, and balance your emotions, working out may be a celebration to you. Any action can be a celebration depending on your intention. The important part is that you tune into what is meaningful for you.

Why it matters

If you are anything like me, you were taught as a kid that some achievements are more important than others. Graduating school, getting good grades, winning a race, and so on… Feats like those are rewarded with parties and praise.

While this is a great way for adults to instill priorities in their kids and help them stay on track, it's not a particularly effective way to help you build your self-esteem or feel accomplished and good about your everyday life, especially if your daily routine doesn't include big moments of glory. It can leave you continually striving for new levels of success, but feeling empty when you achieve them, because it was the reassurance and validation you wanted, not actually the achievement. *Everyday Joy* helps you untangle your sense of self from other people's expectations and gives you the permission to celebrate yourself no matter what the world is telling you about yourself.

When I was in my final position and deciding whether or not to leave the government, I wrestled for a year with what really mattered to me. I loved having an important job that impacted the well-being of the country. But I also felt called to explore other avenues. I wondered if yet another job change would make me feel better or if I needed to leave my career all together. This journal helped me start to separate the parts of me that wanted gold stars and big promotions so I knew I mattered, from the parts of me that wanted to feel valuable for who I was, not for what I did. The more I focused on celebrating my daily life, the clearer I felt about my priorities and values.

When the day came to finally quit, I was still debating accepting a new role working with a team I already knew and loved. I remember walking towards the office where I'd be working; the moment my fingers touched the door handle, I saw an image of myself giggling with children and teaching them laughing yoga. I felt like my heart expanded 10 times in my chest and I knew I had pursue something else. Something that would help me soften and laugh more — and get back in touch with my joy.

Ten plus years later, I have reconnected more deeply with the gentle, playful, loving me at my core. This journal sparked that awakening journey within me, as I hope it will in you too.

The daily celebration — big or small — is your first step in reclaiming your life for yourself. It will help you rewire the old earn-to-achieve reward system you grew up learning, so that you stop withholding your own praise and start honoring your daily achievements and relishing the joy of being you. Even if some days your biggest win is just brushing your teeth or getting dressed!

Tip #3 - Write down your answer first thing in the morning before you leave for the day.

You'll use your *Everyday Joy* journal twice each day — once when you wake up and once before you go to bed. I suggest leaving it on your bedside table so it's easy to remember. I also recommend putting a pen in the book to mark what page you're on so you can find it quickly and easily.

Why it matters

By starting your day with the question of how you will celebrate, you put the inner Labrador Retriever of your mind onto the scent of your joy. Your powerful brain will spend the rest of the day trying to find reasons for you to be happy. This is important if you want to create lasting change and feel happier in the long-term.

Imagine it like a pair of eye glasses. Right now, you're wearing a pair that point out all the annoying, unfair, tedious aspects in your day. Sure, they might be stylish, help you fit in with your friends, or resemble the ones your parents bought you when you were a kid, but they're crappy glasses. They make you feel annoyed and frustrated with life!

Everyday Joy helps you take off those old, frustrating glasses and put on a new, joyful pair that highlight the happiness in your life instead. It may take a while for you to adjust to your new outlook. You may feel like taking a break from your new lens on the world every now and then and wearing old glasses, because you're used to them and they're comfortable. That's okay.

Eventually, your outlook will adjust. You'll stop seeing life the same way you did before and start prioritizing yourself with ease. Soon enough, finding deep pleasure and joy in even the smallest aspects of your life will become your new normal.

Tip #4 - At the end of the day, write down what you actually did to celebrate that day.

Each night, jot down one moment you're celebrating from that day. It may be different than what you anticipated or intended to do; that is okay. In my last year in the government, a colleague and friend used to stop by my desk intermittently and invite me for a walk. Our walks were never planned, so I couldn't anticipate them in my morning celebration journaling. But I counted our walks at the end of the day, because I got outside, moved my body, and connected with a friend. Triple win!

Why it matters

Just like writing down an answer first thing in the morning trains your mind to look for joy all day, remembering a moment of joy trains your mind to scan your memories for joy. It's like reverse claiming. The first time I went through my homemade version of *Everyday Joy*, this was the most surprising, and possibly the most impactful, aspect for me.

I used to think that events in the past were fixed. For example, something would happen, I'd react, and then life would move on. But what I discovered by scanning my day for joy before bed was that *every* memory can be re-painted in a different light.

Say for example, you are wearing your "frustration glasses" during an event. That night at home, you put on your "joy glasses" and think about the event again. With this new perspective, you can have completely different thoughts and feelings about your experience. This is important, because it means that you can go through your entire day focused solely on your to-do list and *still* claim moments of joy in retrospect. In other words, forgetting doesn't mean you're failing.

The best part is that the more you claim your joy retroactively, the more your mind naturally tends to claim everything — even the most mundane parts of your life — as a gift of joy for yourself. Soon every action becomes a celebration and you start to move through your whole day and life nourishing yourself.

Fresh strawberries at lunch? ✓ Delicious.
Quick chat with a colleague walking to a meeting? ✓ Delightful.
Feeling the sunshine through the window? ✓ Heavenly.

Are these moments bubbling over with happiness at the time? Probably not; they are just moments in your day. But looking back and claiming them as a celebration in retrospect helps you realize that small moments like these are opportunities to experience the fullness of your life.

BONUS PROMPTS

Each daily page in *Everyday Joy* also includes two bonus prompts to help you connect with your true essence of joy, honor and relish every day in your life, and expand your self-esteem.

Prompt #1 - Seal your day with gratitude.

This space is for you to jot down what you appreciate and feel grateful for that day. It's okay to repeat the same item across a number of days. The important part is that you truly feel appreciative and grateful as you think of and write it.

Why it matters

Your feelings are your creative superpower as a human. If you imagine yourself as a magnet, your embodied feelings are what magnetizes your life experiences to you. This is why stressed-out people who feel overwhelmed often find themselves faced with more tasks and stress. It's like they're wearing "stress glasses" and only see stress everywhere they look.

That means if you want to feel more present, alive, happy, and connected to yourself, then you need to train yourself to think and feel differently. Your "celebration" glasses are an important first step. Adding appreciation magnifies your results and magnetizes more moments to celebrate into your life.

Prompt #2 - Honor yourself.

The final prompt on your daily journaling page is about what makes you feel proud of yourself. This can include any activity, thoughts, feelings, or experiences you had that day. Anything from keeping your cool in a meeting to meditating to feeling connected with a loved one to walking your daily steps. The important part is that you feel proud of yourself for it.

Now before you tense up remembering all the times you were told as a child not to be arrogant and were shut down with a quick "*No way, you can't do that!*" read on...

Why it matters

For many people, pride has been distorted into arrogance. But pride at its purest is a form of appreciation and gratitude. It is like shining the light of gratitude on yourself.

You may have been taught that being humble means never appreciating or honoring yourself. Now imagine for a moment you need a life-saving surgery. Would you rather use a surgeon who is secure in their skills, aware of their strengths and weaknesses, and confident in their ability to help you? ...Or a surgeon who downplays their abilities, doubts if they have any skill, and feels wrong claiming that they're good at what they do?

I know which one I would choose!

Humans are inherently limited in our abilities; we are not God. But in order to create space for the magic of Source to flow through your life and work, you first have to fully claim the skills and gifts you *do* have. This is the irony of humbleness — to be truly humble in service, you first have to be fully embodied in YOU.

By jotting down a few notes about what you've done, felt, or said that makes you proud of yourself, you are not flaunting your personal power over Life itself; you are embracing the gifts it's giving you. You are honoring your given ability to do the best you can with what you have. That is true service.

If you need more reasons to honor yourself, I've also found that noting what makes me proud helps me reconnect with my values, stay focused on my priorities, and continually hone my intuition.

WEEKLY AND MONTHLY CHECK-INS

At the end of each week and month, you'll find journaling prompts to help you reflect on your favorite moments and celebrate your life more fully. I've also created weekly and monthly guided meditations to help you open to deeper levels of joy and appreciation for yourself and your life. Take a moment right now to download the special meditations and bonus materials that accompany this journal.

You can access them for free at www.becomingyouniversity.com/everyday-joy-gifts.

Why it matters

My life changed using this journaling practice. Unfortunately my experience won't change your life. You have to do that.

The weekly and monthly questions will help you in three main ways:

#1 - Solidify the habit of choosing joy.

Just like putting on your "celebration" glasses at the end of the day helps you claim more moments of joy, revisiting your week and month helps you expand and reaffirm the joys you experienced before. It's one more opportunity to train your mind to seek out joy as a gift for yourself and remember how much joy you actually have in your life. This helps you rewire your mind to honor your everyday experiences of joy, instead of waiting to be happy when you have a big event or milestone.

#2 - Amass evidence you can't deny.

One of the most frustrating cycles I've experienced was wishing all week for the weekend and then resenting how quickly the weekend passed. Your life is happening every day. As I like to say "Tuesday matters too." When you take the time to review how you celebrated your life every day in the past week or month, you are proving to yourself — without a doubt — that you can feel good every day. You don't have to wait for anyone's approval or a momentous occasion. You can be happy right now and enjoy the fullness of your life every day.

#3 - See yourself transforming.

Yours is the only opinion that counts. This could be the most brilliant journal in the world. It could cause the entire population of Earth to discover soul-shaking levels of joy and rework our global systems to encourage more daily happiness. But none of it would matter if you still felt the same.

You are the expert on your life and that means you — and only you — can know how this journal is helping you. You may see changes in your self-esteem, relationships, body image, family dynamics, work-place interactions, and more. The monthly check-ins help you capture your insights, so they don't get overlooked in the daily rush of habitual thinking.

This is how you claim your life back. This is how you retrain your mind to work *for* you. This is how you bring yourself home to joy one day at a time.

3

BEFORE YOU BEGIN

Have you ever wished someone could just wave a wand and you'd feel better? You'd be thinner, richer, happier, clearer, more fun, etc? Me too. But that's not how life works.

Life is experiential. You have to live it to figure out what works for you, feels better or worse, and takes you closer to your goals. On the up-side, that means you have the power to chart your own path towards your desires, success, and happiness. On the down-side, that means you have to be tuned in to your own experience to notice how different choices feel. No numbing out here!

In almost ten years as spiritual mentor helping people live their purpose with clarity, ease, and joy, I've noticed humans are not so skilled at recognizing — or remembering to choose — what makes them feel good. While I could write a whole other book on why that is, suffice to say here that having tangible evidence makes you more likely to use the tools that work for you.

On the next page, you'll find a simple survey to give you a general idea of how you're relating to joy in your life now. Take a moment to fill it out before starting your daily journaling practice.

At the end of your *Everyday Joy* journal, you'll find an identical survey to help you assess your growth over the 90-day journey. Remember, no benefit matters unless it matters to you. There is no perfect or inherently right way to be — only your right way to be you. These surveys will help give you a sense of your own experience so that you can choose more powerfully what helps you feel good and leave behind the rest.

Answer as honestly as you can without overthinking it. No one will see your answers and you won't be graded on them. Trust your gut impulse, since you're only measuring your own feelings. If it helps, bring to mind how you felt over the past week or month as a baseline.

*

In the next chapter, you'll begin your daily joy journaling. If you get stuck or have questions, flip back to Chapter 2, where I share an in-depth description of each journaling question, why it matters, and how it helps. Then you and I will reconnect at the end of Month One to celebrate your progress!

Beginning Survey:

1 is not at all / never 5 is very much / always	1	2	3	4	5
I feel connected to myself					
I make time for myself					
I am generally happy					
I hear & follow my intuition					
I enjoy being alone					
I make time for activities I enjoy					
I have close relationships					
I trust life is working out for me					
My body feels tense and tight					
I frequently feel anxious or worried					
I feel guilty when I relax & do nothing					
I constantly strive to be better					
I am frequently critical & hard on myself					
I get frustrated easily					
I feel exhausted and/or overwhelmed					
I lose my cool in traffic or when late or on hold					

4

YOUR DAILY JOY

First thing in the morning...

Today is the 1ˢᵗ day of the rest of my life. How will I celebrate?

At the end of the day...

How did I celebrate today?

I'm grateful for...

I'm proud of myself for...

First thing in the morning...

Today is the 1ˢᵗ day of the rest of my life. How will I celebrate?

At the end of the day...

How did I celebrate today?

I'm grateful for…

I'm proud of myself for…

"Most folks are about as happy as they make up their minds to be."
- Abraham Lincoln

First thing in the morning...

Today is the 1st day of the rest of my life. How will I celebrate?

At the end of the day...

How did I celebrate today?

I'm grateful for...

I'm proud of myself for...

First thing in the morning...

Today is the 1st day of the rest of my life. How will I celebrate?

At the end of the day...

How did I celebrate today?

I'm grateful for…

I'm proud of myself for…

"What a wonderful life I've had! I only wish I'd realized it sooner."
- Colette

23

First thing in the morning...

Today is the 1st day of the rest of my life. How will I celebrate?

At the end of the day...

How did I celebrate today?

I'm grateful for...

I'm proud of myself for...

First thing in the morning...

Today is the 1ˢᵗ day of the rest of my life. How will I celebrate?

At the end of the day...

How did I celebrate today?

I'm grateful for...

I'm proud of myself for...

"One joy scatters a hundred griefs."
- Chinese Proverb

First thing in the morning...

Today is the 1st day of the rest of my life. How will I celebrate?

At the end of the day...

How did I celebrate today?

I'm grateful for...

I'm proud of myself for...

Weekly Check-in

Download the weekly meditation here: www.becomingyouniversity. com/everyday-joy-gifts.

My favorite celebrations from this past week are...

My most meaningful moments were....

From the past week, I'm most grateful for....

I am most proud of...

Looking forward...

Next week, I am most looking forward to...

First thing in the morning...

Today is the 1st day of the rest of my life. How will I celebrate?

At the end of the day...

How did I celebrate today?

I'm grateful for...

I'm proud of myself for...

First thing in the morning...

Today is the 1st day of the rest of my life. How will I celebrate?

At the end of the day...

How did I celebrate today?

I'm grateful for…

I'm proud of myself for…

"I cling to my imperfection, as the very essence of my being"
- Anatole France

First thing in the morning...

Today is the 1st day of the rest of my life. How will I celebrate?

At the end of the day...

How did I celebrate today?

I'm grateful for…

I'm proud of myself for…

First thing in the morning...

Today is the 1ˢᵗ day of the rest of my life. How will I celebrate?

At the end of the day...

How did I celebrate today?

I'm grateful for...

I'm proud of myself for...

"Great acts are made up of small deeds"
- Lao Tzu

First thing in the morning...

Today is the 1st day of the rest of my life. How will I celebrate?

At the end of the day...

How did I celebrate today?

I'm grateful for...

I'm proud of myself for...

First thing in the morning...

Today is the 1st day of the rest of my life. How will I celebrate?

At the end of the day...

How did I celebrate today?

I'm grateful for...

I'm proud of myself for...

"Worry often gives a small thing a big shadow."
- Swedish proverb

First thing in the morning...

Today is the 1st day of the rest of my life. How will I celebrate?

At the end of the day...

How did I celebrate today?

I'm grateful for...

I'm proud of myself for...

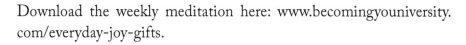

Weekly Check-in

Download the weekly meditation here: www.becomingyouniversity. com/everyday-joy-gifts.

My favorite celebrations from this past week are...

My most meaningful moments were....

From the past week, I'm most grateful for....

I am most proud of...

Looking forward...

Next week, I am most looking forward to...

First thing in the morning...

Today is the 1ˢᵗ day of the rest of my life. How will I celebrate?

At the end of the day...

How did I celebrate today?

I'm grateful for...

I'm proud of myself for...

First thing in the morning...

Today is the 1st day of the rest of my life. How will I celebrate?

At the end of the day...

How did I celebrate today?

I'm grateful for…

I'm proud of myself for…

"There is no happiness like that of being loved by your
fellow creatures, and feeling that your presence
is an addition to their comfort."
- Charlotte Bronte

First thing in the morning...

Today is the 1ˢᵗ day of the rest of my life. How will I celebrate?

At the end of the day...

How did I celebrate today?

I'm grateful for...

I'm proud of myself for...

First thing in the morning...

Today is the 1ˢᵗ day of the rest of my life. How will I celebrate?

At the end of the day...

How did I celebrate today?

I'm grateful for...

I'm proud of myself for...

"What we do belongs to what we are;
and what we are is what becomes of us."
- Henry van Dyke

First thing in the morning...

Today is the 1st day of the rest of my life. How will I celebrate?

At the end of the day...

How did I celebrate today?

I'm grateful for...

I'm proud of myself for...

First thing in the morning...

Today is the 1st day of the rest of my life. How will I celebrate?

At the end of the day...

How did I celebrate today?

I'm grateful for...

I'm proud of myself for...

"Happiness is the meaning and the purpose of life,
the whole aim and end of human existence."
- Aristotle

First thing in the morning...

Today is the 1ˢᵗ day of the rest of my life. How will I celebrate?

At the end of the day...

How did I celebrate today?

I'm grateful for...

I'm proud of myself for...

Weekly Check-in

Download the weekly meditation here: www.becomingyouniversity. com/everyday-joy-gifts.

My favorite celebrations from this past week are...

My most meaningful moments were....

From the past week, I'm most grateful for....

I am most proud of...

Looking forward...

Next week, I am most looking forward to...

First thing in the morning...

Today is the 1st day of the rest of my life. How will I celebrate?

At the end of the day...

How did I celebrate today?

I'm grateful for...

I'm proud of myself for...

First thing in the morning...

Today is the 1st day of the rest of my life. How will I celebrate?

At the end of the day...

How did I celebrate today?

I'm grateful for…

I'm proud of myself for…

"All happiness depends on courage and work."
- Honoré de Balzac

First thing in the morning...

Today is the 1st day of the rest of my life. How will I celebrate?

At the end of the day...

How did I celebrate today?

I'm grateful for...

I'm proud of myself for...

First thing in the morning...

Today is the 1st day of the rest of my life. How will I celebrate?

At the end of the day...

How did I celebrate today?

I'm grateful for...

I'm proud of myself for...

"Who is the happiest of men? He who values the merits of others,
and in their pleasure takes joy, even as though it were his own."
- Johann Wolfgang von Goethe

First thing in the morning...

Today is the 1st day of the rest of my life. How will I celebrate?

At the end of the day...

How did I celebrate today?

I'm grateful for...

I'm proud of myself for...

First thing in the morning...

Today is the 1ˢᵗ day of the rest of my life. How will I celebrate?

At the end of the day...

How did I celebrate today?

I'm grateful for…

I'm proud of myself for…

"The happiness of your life depends upon the quality
of your thoughts: therefore, guard accordingly..."
- Marcus Aurelius

First thing in the morning...

Today is the 1ˢᵗ day of the rest of my life. How will I celebrate?

At the end of the day...

How did I celebrate today?

I'm grateful for…

I'm proud of myself for…

Weekly Check-in

Download the weekly meditation here: www.becomingyouniversity. com/everyday-joy-gifts.

My favorite celebrations from this past week are…

My most meaningful moments were….

From the past week, I'm most grateful for….

I am most proud of…

Looking forward…

Next week, I am most looking forward to…

5

MONTH ONE CHECK-IN

Download the monthly meditation here: www.becomingyouniversity. com/everyday-joy-gifts.

My top celebrations from this past month are…

I am most grateful for….

From the past month, I most proud of...

– Committing to my happiness, completing Month 1, and making it this far!

I'm seeing changes in myself, like...

Celebrating my daily life is impacting me and my life in these ways...

Looking forward...

Next month, I'm most looking forward to...

Congratulations! You completed Month 1!

When I first started celebrating my everyday life, I remember feeling so liberated. It was like I'd found a door to a secret world, where I could feel happy and more in charge of my life no matter what was happening around me. As I continued journaling, I slowly stopped resenting my job as much, too.

My whole life, I'd diligently studied to get a good job. Working a traditional 9-to-5 was a given. But just as I had dutifully pursued that path, I'd also internalized the popular belief that even the best job is still a soul-sucking requirement to survive, and no one would work if they had the choice. A few years into my career that belief had a hold on me, and I felt like my job was robbing me of my "real" life, which happened at nights and on weekends.

Then I started celebrating every day and realizing my power. It was like a light bulb came on! I was *choosing* to work and give my time in exchange for things I valued. Things like stability, money, community, interesting work, and a sense of importance. This aha moment helped me feel more in control of my life. Now when I went to work, no one was *taking* from me, I was freely *giving* my time to benefit in ways that mattered to me.

This simple but meaningful shift helped me discover a new excitement and joy for living. My daily life was still *my* life. I was still choosing how, when, and to what to dedicate *my* precious time. Eventually, this truth led me to leave my government career, because the more I connected with my own power, the more I realized no amount of money or high-ranking job title was enough to justify my time.

So when I share that this one simple daily celebration practice has the potential to change your whole life, I mean it, because it happened to me. But don't worry! You don't have to leave your job or move across the world or even change your daily routine to benefit from your daily celebration practice. Feeling happier and more alive is the biggest outcome of all!

*

To help you expand even further into the joy, support, and possibilities available to you, I want to share with you one of my favorite prayers and invocations.

I like to repeat this one standing with my arms open wide and palms turned up in a gesture of receiving:

"I am open to today being filled with surprises, opportunities, love, joy, and so much more than I can imagine!
I am not limited by my experiences of the past.
Today is a new day and anything is possible when I open my heart!"

Now bring both hands together over the heart and bow your head to your hands:

"Thank you. Thank you. Thank you. And so it is."

Repeat this invocation as often as you'd like to invite even more joy into your life. It's a great one to include in your morning practice to open your heart for your day. If you don't have a morning practice, you can start by standing and saying this.

You can download a printable version of this prayer here: www.becomingyouniversity.com/everyday-joy-gifts.

6

MONTH TWO

First thing in the morning...

Today is the 1st day of the rest of my life. How will I celebrate?

At the end of the day...

How did I celebrate today?

I'm grateful for…

I'm proud of myself for…

First thing in the morning...

Today is the 1st day of the rest of my life. How will I celebrate?

At the end of the day...

How did I celebrate today?

I'm grateful for...

I'm proud of myself for...

"Happiness is like a butterfly which, when pursued, is always beyond our grasp, but, if you will sit down quietly, may alight upon you."
- Nathaniel Hawthorne

First thing in the morning...

Today is the 1ˢᵗ day of the rest of my life. How will I celebrate?

At the end of the day...

How did I celebrate today?

I'm grateful for...

I'm proud of myself for...

First thing in the morning...

Today is the 1ˢᵗ day of the rest of my life. How will I celebrate?

At the end of the day...

How did I celebrate today?

I'm grateful for...

I'm proud of myself for...

"We tend to forget that happiness doesn't come as a result
of getting something we don't have, but rather of recognizing
and appreciating what we do have."
- Frederick Koenig

First thing in the morning...

Today is the 1st day of the rest of my life. How will I celebrate?

At the end of the day...

How did I celebrate today?

I'm grateful for...

I'm proud of myself for...

First thing in the morning...

Today is the 1st day of the rest of my life. How will I celebrate?

At the end of the day...

How did I celebrate today?

I'm grateful for...

I'm proud of myself for...

"Gratitude is the fairest blossom which springs from the soul."
- Henry Ward Beecher

First thing in the morning...

Today is the 1st day of the rest of my life. How will I celebrate?

At the end of the day...

How did I celebrate today?

I'm grateful for...

I'm proud of myself for...

Weekly Check-in

Download the weekly meditation here: www.becomingyouniversity. com/everyday-joy-gifts.

My favorite celebrations from this past week are…

My most meaningful moments were….

From the past week, I'm most grateful for….

I am most proud of…

Looking forward…

Next week, I am most looking forward to…

First thing in the morning...

Today is the 1st day of the rest of my life. How will I celebrate?

At the end of the day...

How did I celebrate today?

I'm grateful for...

I'm proud of myself for...

First thing in the morning...

Today is the 1st day of the rest of my life. How will I celebrate?

At the end of the day...

How did I celebrate today?

I'm grateful for…

I'm proud of myself for…

"The essence of philosophy is that a man should so live that his happiness shall depend as little as possible on external things."
- Epictetus

First thing in the morning...

Today is the 1st day of the rest of my life. How will I celebrate?

At the end of the day...

How did I celebrate today?

I'm grateful for...

I'm proud of myself for...

First thing in the morning...

Today is the 1st day of the rest of my life. How will I celebrate?

At the end of the day...

How did I celebrate today?

I'm grateful for...

I'm proud of myself for...

"Use what talents you possess; the woods would be very silent if no birds sang except those that sang best."
- Henry van Dyke

First thing in the morning...

Today is the 1st day of the rest of my life. How will I celebrate?

At the end of the day...

How did I celebrate today?

I'm grateful for…

I'm proud of myself for…

First thing in the morning...

Today is the 1st day of the rest of my life. How will I celebrate?

At the end of the day...

How did I celebrate today?

I'm grateful for…

I'm proud of myself for…

"Drag your thoughts away from your troubles — by the ears, by the
heels, or any other way, so you manage it."
- Mark Twain

First thing in the morning...

Today is the 1st day of the rest of my life. How will I celebrate?

At the end of the day...

How did I celebrate today?

I'm grateful for...

I'm proud of myself for...

Weekly Check-in

Download the weekly meditation here: www.becomingyouniversity.com/everyday-joy-gifts.

My favorite celebrations from this past week are…

My most meaningful moments were….

From the past week, I'm most grateful for….

I am most proud of…

Looking forward…

Next week, I am most looking forward to…

First thing in the morning...

Today is the 1st day of the rest of my life. How will I celebrate?

At the end of the day...

How did I celebrate today?

I'm grateful for…

I'm proud of myself for…

First thing in the morning...

Today is the 1st day of the rest of my life. How will I celebrate?

At the end of the day...

How did I celebrate today?

I'm grateful for…

I'm proud of myself for…

"Happiness is not an ideal of reason, but of imagination."
- Immanuel Kant

First thing in the morning...

Today is the 1ˢᵗ day of the rest of my life. How will I celebrate?

At the end of the day...

How did I celebrate today?

I'm grateful for…

I'm proud of myself for…

First thing in the morning...

Today is the 1ˢᵗ day of the rest of my life. How will I celebrate?

At the end of the day...

How did I celebrate today?

I'm grateful for…

I'm proud of myself for…

"Happiness is where we find it, but very rarely where we seek it."
- J. Petit Senn

First thing in the morning...

Today is the 1st day of the rest of my life. How will I celebrate?

At the end of the day...

How did I celebrate today?

I'm grateful for…

I'm proud of myself for…

First thing in the morning...

Today is the 1st day of the rest of my life. How will I celebrate?

At the end of the day...

How did I celebrate today?

I'm grateful for...

I'm proud of myself for...

"Happiness is not a goal; it is a by-product."
- Eleanor Roosevelt

First thing in the morning...

Today is the 1ˢᵗ day of the rest of my life. How will I celebrate?

At the end of the day...

How did I celebrate today?

I'm grateful for…

I'm proud of myself for…

Weekly Check-in

Download the weekly meditation here: www.becomingyouniversity.com/everyday-joy-gifts.

My favorite celebrations from this past week are…

My most meaningful moments were….

From the past week, I'm most grateful for….

I am most proud of…

Looking forward…

Next week, I am most looking forward to…

First thing in the morning...

Today is the 1st day of the rest of my life. How will I celebrate?

At the end of the day...

How did I celebrate today?

I'm grateful for…

I'm proud of myself for…

First thing in the morning...

Today is the 1st day of the rest of my life. How will I celebrate?

At the end of the day...

How did I celebrate today?

I'm grateful for...

I'm proud of myself for...

"True happiness is not attained through self-gratification,
but through fidelity to a worthy purpose."
- Helen Keller

First thing in the morning...

Today is the 1st day of the rest of my life. How will I celebrate?

At the end of the day...

How did I celebrate today?

I'm grateful for...

I'm proud of myself for...

First thing in the morning...

Today is the 1st day of the rest of my life. How will I celebrate?

At the end of the day...

How did I celebrate today?

I'm grateful for…

I'm proud of myself for…

"I must learn to be content with being happier than I deserve."
- Jane Austen

First thing in the morning...

Today is the 1st day of the rest of my life. How will I celebrate?

At the end of the day...

How did I celebrate today?

I'm grateful for...

I'm proud of myself for...

First thing in the morning...

Today is the 1st day of the rest of my life. How will I celebrate?

At the end of the day...

How did I celebrate today?

I'm grateful for…

I'm proud of myself for…

*"He who lives in harmony with himself
lives in harmony with the universe."*
- Marcus Aurelius

First thing in the morning...

Today is the 1ˢᵗ day of the rest of my life. How will I celebrate?

At the end of the day...

How did I celebrate today?

I'm grateful for…

I'm proud of myself for…

Weekly Check-in

Download the weekly meditation here: www.becomingyouniversity. com/everyday-joy-gifts.

My favorite celebrations from this past week are…

My most meaningful moments were….

From the past week, I'm most grateful for….

I am most proud of…

Looking forward…

Next week, I am most looking forward to…

7

MONTH TWO CHECK-IN

Download the monthly meditation here: www.becomingyouniversity.com/everyday-joy-gifts.

My top celebrations from this past month are…

I am most grateful for….

From the past month, I most proud of...

- Committing to my happiness, completing Month 1, and making it this far!

I'm seeing changes in myself, like...

Celebrating my daily life is impacting me and my life in these ways...

Looking forward...

Next month, I'm most looking forward to...

Wow! You completed 2 months of joy journalling!

C ongratulations! I hope by now you're starting to see positive changes in your life. They may be subtle and small at first, so stay open and expect the best!

When I first created this journal, I was surprised by some of the shifts I noticed. My goal was to feel like my life mattered every day and wasn't being wished away pining for the weekend, so it was an added bonus to see other results too.

For example, I noticed that I started to eat more fruit and also stopped over-eating sweets and junk food as much. Since I was savoring these treats as gifts for myself in my daily celebration, I enjoyed them more mindfully. I also started walking more. Because I wrote things like walks and fruit in both the daily celebration and *I'm proud of myself for...* list, each one gave me double joy. I got to feel good while doing it and then also while thinking about it afterwards!

*

Most changes you may notice are small, but not all of them are seamless and easy. When change involves other people, you can experience an adjustment period as you both grow into a new dynamic. That's a nice way of saying things can feel pretty rough for a while.

As I kept journaling, I started speaking up more for my thoughts and desires. Without realizing it, I had allowed other people's expectations and beliefs to determine my actions. Whether it was my boss, a boyfriend, or my parents, I discovered I'd been making a lot of decisions in an effort to make other people happy, so that I would feel safe and loved.

The more I celebrated my life, the more I discovered myself. As I did, I realized my dreams didn't always align with my reality. For example, I had a secure, well-paying job in the government, but that was actually my tenured-professor Dad's dream for me. Of course, he wanted his little girl to be settled and safe!

These discoveries meant that voicing my desires and opinions was about more than just speaking my truth. It was also about feeling safe, loved, and connected to others. These dynamics aren't as easy to evolve overnight as simply drinking more water or eating more fruit. They touch into a deeper thread of emotion that runs through your life and shapes how you see yourself and others.

I invite you to gift yourself patience, understanding, and compassion as you reveal new truths within yourself through this journaling process. It helps me to remember that our old beliefs and habits stemmed from a genuine desire to be safe and loved. Now we just have better tools and knowledge to chose more healthy and supportive ways of being!

Take heart that the more you celebrate yourself and your life, the clearer you will be about who you are and how you want to be. Then you'll able to communicate your priorities more easily, while still staying connected to the well of joy, love, and compassion within you.

Lastly, know you are not alone. Life itself is standing by to help you become who you are meant to be. Change doesn't have to be hard or unsettling. As energy healer Deana Welch says, "Ain't no one got time for a healing crisis!" You can ask Life to ease the transition for you.

*

This is one of my favorite prayers to zoom out my perspective and stay focused on what really matters — feeling like an active participant in my own life.

Place one hand over your heart and the other on your belly and say aloud:

"Dear Creator of all that is and Source of love and endless possibilities,
Please free me from being who I think I have to be to meet other people's
expectations.
Free me to know my own truth.
Return me now to my essence.
I claim my sovereign power.
I am my sovereign power.
I am!"

And so it is.

Download a printable version of this prayer here: www.becomingyouniversity.com/everyday-joy-gifts.

8

MONTH THREE

First thing in the morning...

Today is the 1st day of the rest of my life. How will I celebrate?

At the end of the day...

How did I celebrate today?

I'm grateful for...

I'm proud of myself for...

First thing in the morning...

Today is the 1st day of the rest of my life. How will I celebrate?

At the end of the day...

How did I celebrate today?

I'm grateful for…

I'm proud of myself for…

"For every minute you are angry, you lose sixty seconds of happiness"
- Ralph Waldo Emerson

First thing in the morning...

Today is the 1ˢᵗ day of the rest of my life. How will I celebrate?

At the end of the day...

How did I celebrate today?

I'm grateful for…

I'm proud of myself for…

First thing in the morning...

Today is the 1st day of the rest of my life. How will I celebrate?

At the end of the day...

How did I celebrate today?

I'm grateful for…

I'm proud of myself for…

"The true secret of happiness lies in taking a genuine interest
in all the details of daily life."
- William Morris

First thing in the morning...

Today is the 1st day of the rest of my life. How will I celebrate?

At the end of the day...

How did I celebrate today?

I'm grateful for…

I'm proud of myself for…

First thing in the morning...

Today is the 1st day of the rest of my life. How will I celebrate?

At the end of the day...

How did I celebrate today?

I'm grateful for…

I'm proud of myself for…

"There is only one happiness in this life, to love and be loved."
- George Sand

First thing in the morning...

Today is the 1ˢᵗ day of the rest of my life. How will I celebrate?

At the end of the day...

How did I celebrate today?

I'm grateful for...

I'm proud of myself for...

Weekly Check-in

Download the weekly meditation here: www.becomingyouniversity.com/everyday-joy-gifts.

My favorite celebrations from this past week are…

My most meaningful moments were….

From the past week, I'm most grateful for….

I am most proud of…

Looking forward…

Next week, I am most looking forward to…

First thing in the morning...

Today is the 1st day of the rest of my life. How will I celebrate?

At the end of the day...

How did I celebrate today?

I'm grateful for...

I'm proud of myself for...

First thing in the morning...

Today is the 1st day of the rest of my life. How will I celebrate?

At the end of the day...

How did I celebrate today?

I'm grateful for…

I'm proud of myself for…

"The happiness of life is made up of the little charities of
a kiss or smile, a kind look, a heartfelt compliment."
- Samuel Taylor Coleridge

First thing in the morning...

Today is the 1st day of the rest of my life. How will I celebrate?

At the end of the day...

How did I celebrate today?

I'm grateful for...

I'm proud of myself for...

First thing in the morning...

Today is the 1st day of the rest of my life. How will I celebrate?

At the end of the day...

How did I celebrate today?

I'm grateful for…

I'm proud of myself for…

"Happiness is not a matter of events,
it depends upon the tides of the mind"
- Alice Meynell

First thing in the morning...

Today is the 1st day of the rest of my life. How will I celebrate?

At the end of the day...

How did I celebrate today?

I'm grateful for…

I'm proud of myself for…

First thing in the morning...

Today is the 1st day of the rest of my life. How will I celebrate?

At the end of the day...

How did I celebrate today?

I'm grateful for…

I'm proud of myself for…

"To get up each morning with the resolve to be happy... is to set our own conditions to the events of each day. To do this is to condition circumstances instead of being conditioned by them."
- Ralph Waldo Emerson

First thing in the morning...

Today is the 1st day of the rest of my life. How will I celebrate?

At the end of the day...

How did I celebrate today?

I'm grateful for...

I'm proud of myself for...

Weekly Check-in

Download the weekly meditation here: www.becomingyouniversity.com/everyday-joy-gifts.

My favorite celebrations from this past week are…

My most meaningful moments were….

From the past week, I'm most grateful for….

I am most proud of…

Looking forward…

Next week, I am most looking forward to…

First thing in the morning...

Today is the 1st day of the rest of my life. How will I celebrate?

At the end of the day...

How did I celebrate today?

I'm grateful for...

I'm proud of myself for...

First thing in the morning...

Today is the 1st day of the rest of my life. How will I celebrate?

At the end of the day...

How did I celebrate today?

I'm grateful for...

I'm proud of myself for...

"Now and then it's good to pause in our pursuit of
happiness and just be happy."
- Guillaume Apollinaire

First thing in the morning...

Today is the 1st day of the rest of my life. How will I celebrate?

At the end of the day...

How did I celebrate today?

I'm grateful for...

I'm proud of myself for...

First thing in the morning...

Today is the 1st day of the rest of my life. How will I celebrate?

At the end of the day...

How did I celebrate today?

I'm grateful for…

I'm proud of myself for…

"Happiness grows at our own firesides, and is not
to be picked in stranger's gardens."
- Douglas Jerrold

First thing in the morning...

Today is the 1st day of the rest of my life. How will I celebrate?

At the end of the day...

How did I celebrate today?

I'm grateful for...

I'm proud of myself for...

First thing in the morning...

Today is the 1st day of the rest of my life. How will I celebrate?

At the end of the day...

How did I celebrate today?

I'm grateful for…

I'm proud of myself for…

"Action may not always bring happiness;
but there is no happiness without action."
- Benjamin Disraeli

First thing in the morning...

Today is the 1ˢᵗ day of the rest of my life. How will I celebrate?

At the end of the day...

How did I celebrate today?

I'm grateful for...

I'm proud of myself for...

Weekly Check-in

Download the weekly meditation here: www.becomingyouniversity.com/everyday-joy-gifts.

My favorite celebrations from this past week are…

My most meaningful moments were….

From the past week, I'm most grateful for….

I am most proud of…

Looking forward…

Next week, I am most looking forward to…

First thing in the morning...

Today is the 1ˢᵗ day of the rest of my life. How will I celebrate?

At the end of the day...

How did I celebrate today?

I'm grateful for…

I'm proud of myself for…

First thing in the morning...

Today is the 1st day of the rest of my life. How will I celebrate?

At the end of the day...

How did I celebrate today?

I'm grateful for…

I'm proud of myself for…

"Happiness depends more on the inward disposition of mind than on outward circumstances."
- Benjamin Franklin

First thing in the morning...

Today is the 1ˢᵗ day of the rest of my life. How will I celebrate?

At the end of the day...

How did I celebrate today?

I'm grateful for...

I'm proud of myself for...

First thing in the morning...

Today is the 1st day of the rest of my life. How will I celebrate?

At the end of the day...

How did I celebrate today?

I'm grateful for…

I'm proud of myself for…

"No man is happy who does not think himself so."
- Publilius Syrus

First thing in the morning...

Today is the 1st day of the rest of my life. How will I celebrate?

At the end of the day...

How did I celebrate today?

I'm grateful for...

I'm proud of myself for...

First thing in the morning...

Today is the 1st day of the rest of my life. How will I celebrate?

At the end of the day...

How did I celebrate today?

I'm grateful for…

I'm proud of myself for…

"Happiness resides not in possessions, and not in gold,
happiness dwells in the soul."
- Democritus

First thing in the morning...

Today is the 1st day of the rest of my life. How will I celebrate?

At the end of the day...

How did I celebrate today?

I'm grateful for…

I'm proud of myself for…

Weekly Check-in

Download the weekly meditation here: www.becomingyouniversity. com/everyday-joy-gifts.

My favorite celebrations from this past week are...

My most meaningful moments were....

From the past week, I'm most grateful for....

I am most proud of...

Looking forward...

Next week, I am most looking forward to...

9

MONTH THREE CHECK-IN

Download the monthly meditation here: www.becomingyouniversity.com/everyday-joy-gifts.

My top celebrations from this past month are…

I am most grateful for….

From the past month, I most proud of...

- Committing to my happiness, completing Month 1, and making it this far!

I'm seeing changes in myself, like...

Celebrating my daily life is impacting me and my life in these ways...

Looking forward...

Next month, I'm most looking forward to...

Congratulations!

You did it! You completed 90-days of joy journaling! Before moving onto the Closing Survey and next steps, I invite you to spend a few moments in reflective celebration.

Place one hand on your heart and one hand on your belly, and gift these words to yourself:

"I create joy in my every day life.
I open my mind, body, and spirit to ever-increasing joy and happiness.
My life is a gift, and I celebrate that gift daily.
Thank you for the joy of living.
Thank you for the joy of being me.
I embrace myself fully now and always.
Thank you."

Bow your head to your heart and thank yourself for the time you dedicated to yourself and to this daily celebration practice. You are a true champion for your joy and ally to your soul.

On the following page, write down any hopes and wishes for yourself and your life that you may be holding in your heart.

How do you most want to feel?
What meaningful experiences do you want to create?
How does happiness feel in your body?
What truths do you hope to remember about life and yourself?

You may also enjoy drawing your vision and feelings. These words and images are like guideposts to your future. They symbolize the life you are creating and who you are becoming, so allow yourself to dream big!

10

MARKING YOUR TRANSFORMATION

You've done the work — now it's time to integrate your results more deeply with the closing survey. This step is important, because your experience is your best guide to creating a joy-filled life. No tool or technique matters if it doesn't help you feel, think, and be how *you* want to feel, think, and be. In other words: no benefit matters unless it matters to you. There is no perfect or right way to be — only *your* right way to be *you*.

In Chapter 3, you (hopefully) filled out the Beginning Survey before starting your 90-day joy journaling process. Now you'll retake the same survey and see what changes you notice. This is not a test and you cannot fail. It's just one more way to understand and explore your own experience, so that you know what supports you in becoming who you want to be.

Take a minute right now to fill out the survey on the next page. Then revisit Chapter 3 and compare your answers. Like taking your temperature, your answers are only meaningful in reference to your previous answers.

What changes do you notice?

If you see positive movement, keep up your daily celebration journaling; it's clearly working for you! But if a negative feeling increased, explore the reasons why.

- *Are you feeling stronger in yourself and thus less patient with old habits and patterns?*
- *Are you clearer in your boundaries and so less tolerant of some of the dynamics in your life?*
- *Are you more aware of your emotions and how your body feels and therefore feeling more sensitive to subtle changes?*
- *Are you resisting actually feeling happy, proud, or grateful in your body and instead just going through the motions?*

Sometimes when we make a change on a deep level, it can stir up our emotions as the old patterns start releasing, but we don't yet have new and empowering habits to take their place. Imagine it like kicking up muck on the bottom of a lake. The water temporarily gets cloudy as the combination of sand, dirt, and leaves float around until they slowly settle into a new foundation.

The same can be true for you. When you shift how you feel about yourself and how you interact with life on a fundamental level, all of the old ways you used to think, feel, and act also get stirred up. In my experience, there's a transitional period, during which you still have all the old habits, but now you have a new awareness too. That can make you feel like you're losing your mind! Because now you see yourself more clearly, but you might not yet have the new skills and tools to approach life in a different way.

Have faith if you're feeling more frustrated or short-tempered with yourself and others, or even more aware of pain and tension in your body. It can take time to settle into your new way of being and feel clear, calm, and centered in your joy. Keep practicing your daily celebration.

You have the power to chart your own path towards your best life. This survey and what you discover through your answers can help you figure out what steps bring you closer to your goals. But only you can start walking.

Closing Survey:

1 is not at all / never 5 is very much / always	1	2	3	4	5
I feel connected to myself					
I make time for myself					
I am generally happy					
I hear & follow my intuition					
I enjoy being alone					
I make time for activities I enjoy					
I have close relationships					
I trust life is working out for me					
My body feels tense and tight					
I frequently feel anxious or worried					
I feel guilty when I relax & do nothing					
I constantly strive to be better					
I am frequently critical & hard on myself					
I get frustrated easily					
I feel exhausted and/or overwhelmed					
I lose my cool in traffic or when late or on hold					

11

NOW WHAT?

I'm so proud of you for finishing the journal! 100 gold stars from me! The important part is that you dedicated the time and awareness to yourself and becoming who you want to be.

So, now what?

Here are a few options that will support you moving forward:

#1 - Keep going!

Just because this journal is complete doesn't mean you can't start a new one. Order another or keep up your daily celebration in your own journal. The top priority is continuing to claim your life today, instead of waiting for someday to finally live.

#2 - Share to deepen

Sharing is one of the most powerful tools we have as humans have to amplify our own understanding and embrace new discoveries. That's why so many people end up talking and teaching about what helps them. The same is true for you, too. Sharing this journal will help you deepen more fully into your joy and daily celebrating. Plus you'll create a community of confident, happy, sovereign souls around you to support you in your journey!

#3 - Connect with me in the online hub

If you haven't already, join us here: www.becomingyouniversity.com/everyday-joy-gifts. When you join, you'll be first on the list to hear about new opportunities, as well as gain access to meditations, downloadable prayers, and other bonuses. You'll also be able to ask me questions and share your success stories to be featured.

Final words of inspiration

Your daily celebration practice has given you a head start towards creating a genuinely meaningful, happy life. You now have the power to strengthen your self-esteem, prioritize yourself, and rewire your brain — as well as your whole life — for joy. All from celebrating your everyday existence!

Keep going. Other people in your life may still be stuck trying to patch their fears and insecurities in unhelpful ways. They may be looking to promotions, food, or fancy clothes to make themselves feel important.

But you know the truth: Your happiness comes from within.

I invite you to continue this journey with me and step into new levels of clarity and ease as you embrace yourself and your purpose. Nothing is more important than fully becoming you. I am dedicated to helping you connect with the truth of who you are and come home to the bliss of being you.

Discover more and join me at http://alexispierce.com/.

A prayer of remembering:

I am not my limitations.
I am not my distorted thoughts.
I am not the opinions of others or the shapes I've contorted myself into
to receive acceptance, safety, and love.
I am not my worst fears.
I am not my worries and insecurities.
I am not who I was or who people expect and tell me to be.

I am me.

Whole. Pure. Radiant. Perfectly me.
I am a divine reflection of Source itself,
Infinite in my power and boundless in my possibilities.
I am truth embodied.
I am love embodied.
I am sacred, and I hold myself to be sacred now.

Thank you for bringing me home to my truth.
Thank you for bringing me home to my body.
Thank you for bringing my home to my soul.

I am me.

ABOUT THE AUTHOR

A lexis Pierce is an award-winning strategist and soul purpose expert who guides people to discover and embody clarity, peace, and purpose. She spent years as a strategist in the U.S. government advising U.S. Ambassadors, foreign dignitaries, the White House, and members of Congress. Now, she combines that same expertise with over a decade of yoga and meditation teaching to help you create your own ideal life.

Her work has been featured in publications including Authority Magazine, The Huffington Post, Medium, YFS Magazine, MindBody Green, Thrive Global, and referenced on Success Magazine's online home Success.com. Alexis holds degrees from the University of Chicago and Georgetown University, and received a Certificate from the Yale Executive Education Program in Business Strategy and Planning. She currently lives in Central New York, with her husband and two dogs.

Her next book on knowing and living your soul's calling is forthcoming. You can learn more and sign up for her newsletter at www. alexispierce.com

Made in the USA
Middletown, DE
17 September 2023

38516860R00087